ALSO BY DAVID MALOUF

Fiction
Johnno
Fly Away Peter
Child's Play
Harland's Half Acre
Antipodes
The Great World
Remembering Babylon
The Conversations at Curlow Creek
Dream Stuff
Every Move You Make
The Complete Stories
Ransom

Autobiography
12 Edmondstone Street

Poetry
"Interiors" in Four Poets
Bicycle and Other Poems
Neighbours in a Thicket
Poems 1976–7
The Year of the Foxes and Other Poems
First Things Last
Wild Lemons
Selected Poems
Typewriter Music
Revolving Days

Plays
Blood Relations

Libretti
Voss
Baa Baa Black Sheep
Jane Eyre

THE HAPPY LIFE

THE HAPPY LIFE

*The Search for Contentment
in the Modern World*

DAVID MALOUF

Pantheon Books, New York

Library of Congress Cataloging-in-Publication Data
Malouf, David, [date]
The happy life : the search for contentment in the modern world /
David Malouf.
    p.   cm.
Includes bibliographical references (p   ).
ISBN 978-0-307-90771-4
1. Happiness. 2. Contentment. I. Title.

BJ1481.M3188 2012   170—dc23   2012007180

www.pantheonbooks.com

Jacket design by Emily Mahon

Printed in the United States of America
First United States Edition
2   4   6   8   9   7   5   3   1

Contents

THE HAPPY LIFE

The Character of a Happy Life

Happiness surely is among the simplest of human emotions and the most spontaneous. There can be no one, however miserable the conditions of their daily existence, who has not at some time felt the joy of being alive in the moment; in the love of another, or the closeness of friends or fellow workers; in a baby's smile, the satisfaction of a job well done or the first green in a winter furrow; or more simply still, bird-song or the touch of sunlight. But for the vast majority of men and women who have shared our planet in the long course of human history, these can have been no more than moments in a life that was unremittingly harsh.

Think of a medieval farmer as he struggled to keep body and soul together, at the mercy of famine, plague and the periodic arrival over the horizon of mercenaries in search of food or plunder; or women and children in the eighteenth century who spent fifteen hours a day hauling a truck loaded with coal out of a pit; or the African slaves who endured the Middle Passage to the Americas. Think of the millions, soldiers and civilians both, caught up in the wars and social upheavals of the last century, the invasions, evacuations, forced resettlements, the daily struggle to survive the horrors of Auschwitz-Birkenau or Belsen or Mauthausen.

We get some idea of what "happy" might mean to an inmate of the Soviet Gulags from the list of small mercies at the end of Alexander Solzhenitsyn's *One Day in the Life of Ivan Denisovich*:

> Shukhov went off to sleep, and he was completely content. Fate had been kind to him in many ways that day: he hadn't been put in the cells, the gang had not been sent to the Socialist Community Centre, he'd fiddled himself an extra bowl of porridge for dinner, the gang-leader had fixed a good percentage, he'd been happy building that wall, he'd slipped through the search with that bit of blade, he'd earned himself something from Tsesar in the evening, he'd bought his tobacco. And he hadn't fallen ill—had overcome his feelings of illness in the morning.
>
> The day had gone by without a single cloud—almost a happy day.
>
> There were three thousand six hundred and fifty-three days like that in his sentence, from reveille to lights out.
>
> The three extra days were because of the leap years . . .[1]

The truth is that for most of our history only the few, who had the privilege of living free of long hours of hard labour and vulnerability to privation and every form of accident, enjoyed the luxury of considering what happiness of a more settled kind might be: the freedom to cultivate, outside the turmoil of daily living, their "garden." Either a real one of orchards and shady walks—Horace's Sabine farm or Voltaire's Ferney—or the metaphorical one of Marvell's "green thought in a green shade." Or, within a life that is still engaged with contingency and dailyness, what Montaigne calls "the little back-shop, all our own, entirely free," that we must set aside for our self-preservation in even the most crowded household. "In this retreat," he tells us,

> we should keep up our ordinary converse with our-selves, and so private, that no acquaintance or outside communication may find a place there; there to talk and laugh, as if we had neither wife, nor children, nor worldly goods, retinue or servants; to the end that, should we happen to lose them, it may be no new thing to do without them . . . Since God gives us permission to arrange for our own removal, let us prepare for it; let us pack up our belongings, take leave betimes of the company, and shake off those violent holdfasts that engage us elsewhere and estrange us from ourselves. We must undo those powerful bonds, and from this day forth we may love this and that, but be wedded only to ourselves. That is to say, let the rest be ours, but not joined and glued so firmly to us that it cannot be detached without taking our skin along with it, and tearing away a piece of us. The greatest thing in the world is to know how to belong to yourself.[2]

Montaigne knows only too well, of course, that one needs more than "God's permission" to achieve this. It helps if one is also the Seigneur de Montaigne, *Chevalier de l'ordre du Roy et Gentilhomme ordinaire de sa chambre*, mayor and governor of Bordeaux, a child of fortune and high privilege; though even then one will be as vulnerable as any other to the ills of the body, and to the hesitations, doubts, irrational hauntings, moods, fears that trouble our fragile consciousness; and of course no one, however protected by royal favour and titles, is safe from Death.

Behind Montaigne's very idiosyncratic avocation of the "little back-shop" of domestic retirement lies a tradition that reaches deep into the classical past: to Seneca, Cicero, Epictetus, and beyond those later writers to Epicurus, Aristotle and Plato in the fourth century BC. This is the tradition we catch a late echo of in one of the most admired of seventeenth-century English poems, Sir Henry Wotton's "Character of a Happy Life," a version of Horace's *Second Epode,* "Beatus ille qui"—*"Happy he who . . ."*[3]:

> How happy is he born or taught
>   That serveth not another's will;
> Whose armour is his honest thought,
>   And silly truth his highest skill!

Whose passions not his masters are,
　　Whose soul is still prepared for death;
Untied unto the world with care
　　Of princely love or vulgar breath;

Who hath his life from rumours freed,
　　Whose conscience is his strong retreat;
Whose state can neither flatterers feed,
　　Nor ruin make accusers great;

Who envieth none whom chance doth raise
　　Or vice; who never understood
How deepest wounds are given with praise;
　　Nor rules of state, but rules of good;

Who God doth late and early pray
　　More of his grace than gifts to lend;
Who entertains the harmless day
　　With a well-chosen book or friend;

—This man is free from servile bands
　　Of hope to rise, or fear to fall;
Lord of himself, though not of lands;
　　And having nothing, he hath all.[4]

　　Wotton, an intimate of John Donne at Oxford and later of the greatest scholar of the age, Isaac Casaubon at Geneva, is in many ways the model of a Renaissance man. The life he celebrates in his poem is his own. It strikes a balance between those opposing possibilities, as the age saw it, of the active and the contemplative life. He spent thirty years in the diplomatic service and had a wit that sometimes got him into trouble; he was responsible for the cheeky definition of a diplomat as "an honest man sent to lie abroad for the good of his country." He was for more than twenty years the British ambassador at Venice and in retirement, as Provost of Eton, spent his days, "harmlessly" as he puts it, in the company of his books and a few close friends, but also fishing in a bend of the Thames known as the Black Potts. His companion on these occasions was Izaak Walton, who later described their days together in his *Compleat Angler*.

Wotton, as all this suggests, was a man of the world and knew only too well its ways. How high office attracts empty flatterers but also men whose chief concern is to slander and bring you down. How words that are meant to kill can disguise themselves as praise. How the man of prestige and even the smallest power can waste his spirit in dreams of greater power or fear of fall. Wotton himself is a model of Montaigne's insistence that "Solitude is more becoming and more reasonable in one who gives to the world the most active and most vigorous period of his life."[5] Having embraced the world of action and affairs with all the energy that was in him, he also managed to hold himself apart from its temptations to corruption, both of the public and of the private sort, and, dependent neither on the approval of princes nor of the mob, remained one who, to the end, was "Lord of himself, though not of lands, and having nothing, he hath all." We have no nicer statement in later times of what the various classical schools, the Aristotelean, the Epicurean, the Stoic, would have agreed was the highest form of happiness, but also the highest wisdom.

And these days?

One difference, at least in developed societies like our own—and it is a large one—is that something called happiness is a condition that we all aspire to, and which, whatever our place in society, we see it as our right to enjoy. We judge a society, and the state that is based upon it, by how free and happy its people are, and the extent to which its institutions provide for that possibility. Jeremy Bentham's proposition in *An Introduction to the Principles of Morals and Legislation* (1789)— "the greatest happiness for the greatest number"—has become essential to any serious political platform.

But what, in our understanding of the word, does happiness actually mean, and how did it come to be seen as a *right,* a possibility that should be available to all? And how does "the happy life" as we conceive it now, at the end of the first decade of the twenty-first century—in a world where "happy pills" can be purchased on prescription, or at any dance party or club, when every city bar has its Happy Hour and one of the instant cures for low-level *un*happiness is what we call "retail therapy"—relate to the way Aristotle, or Seneca, or even Montaigne saw it, or as it appeared to Sir Henry Wotton?

The happy life for Wotton was the life that made full use of the gifts a man had been given, that fulfilled its promise, first in action, then in days and nights of rest; life had been good to him, but he had also served it well in return. Asked about the "good" life, he might have pointed to that word "harmless." He had done what he could for the world and done no man harm.

The "good life" as we understand it today does not raise the question of how we have lived, of moral qualities or usefulness or harm; we no longer use the phrase in that way. The good life as we understand it has to do with what we call lifestyle, with living it up in a world that offers us gifts or goodies free for the taking. In terms that even the early twentieth century might have understood, the notion of Virtue barely exists for us. It is a quaint, old-fashioned word that in the daily busyness of living, like its counterpart, Evil, has no useful currency. Evil exists, as cancer does. It is mysterious, scary and we have no cure for it, but we see it as specific rather than general. Ordinary men and women can be foolish, inconsiderate, irresponsible, selfish, greedy; irrational anger and fear, or drugs and alcohol, can make them do things that are destructive and criminal. They are not necessarily evil. But there are others of us—they are statistically few—who have no sense of the reality of others or of the feelings of others. Neuroscientists would tell us that they are the victims of a chemical condition. This, for the moment, seems to be as far as we can go.

In the world of behaviour to which virtue once referred we think of *social* qualities now as constituting the terms in which goodness presents itself: goodness of heart, public-spiritedness, generosity, charity, concern for others—community values, which is no bad thing; neighbourliness, the responsibility we feel to the general good, our contribution to the world at large; the contributions we make to the needs of others.

Television is full of advertisements and appeals to our social conscience and goodwill: Save the Children, World Vision, Oxfam, Médecins sans Frontières, Amnesty International; at a local level the St. Vincent de Paul Society and the Salvation Army. We leave the private choices, questions of sexual behaviour, for example, to personal disposition, unless it takes a social form as domestic violence or a legal one as child abuse. If the attainment of spiritual equanimity is a question at all, it is for the individual to pursue as a private matter.

The consolations of philosophy are still available to us, as they were to Montaigne, in the writings of Plato, Aristotle, Epictetus, Cicero, Seneca; and in these early decades of the twenty-first century, we can also turn to Montaigne himself, and to Spinoza, Kant, Schopenhauer, Kierkegaard. But we have no formal schools, such as the Greeks and Romans had, for training their elite in personal and social discipline; in care of the self—its preservation, that is, against vulnerability to externals, against loss of self-containment and self-sufficiency, loss of control.

What we have is psychological help for those who seek it, or the pastoral care of a church if we belong to one; or yoga, meditation, dating agencies, Facebook, Gaydar, drugs, cycling or jogging; or the full range of stimulus and sensation provided by continuous sporting programs on pay TV, endlessly proliferating porn websites, Fashion or Race or Food weeks, or all-night clubs. It's a free world, make your choice.

Most of us these days enjoy the good life in this later, material sense. (I say "most of us," but I mean the new privileged, those of us who live in advanced, industrial societies. The truth is that though we are all alive on the planet in the same moment, we are not all living in the same century.)

We are also, if we are to judge from the high level of volunteerism in the community, living good lives—in the later sense of lives that take clear account of others, the less fortunate, and in our readiness to devote so much of our time and leisure to being useful, to "contributing."

The question that arises is not so much "How should we live if we want to be happy?" but how is it, when the chief sources of human *un*happiness, of misery and wretchedness, have largely been removed from our lives—large-scale social injustice, famine, plague and other diseases, the near-certainty of an early death—that happiness still eludes so many of us? What have we succumbed to or failed to do that might have helped us? What is it in us, or in the world we have created, that continues to hold us back?

"The Pursuit of Happiness"

On a hot summer's day in June 1776, in a room on the second floor of a three-storey house at the corner of Market and Seventh streets on the outskirts of Philadelphia, the thirty-three-year-old Thomas Jefferson sat down to the task he had been assigned of writing the declaration that would proclaim the separation of his country, the future United States of America, from Great Britain.

He had a good idea of the importance of what he was doing, and the language he adopts is as grand as the occasion, in his vision of it, was momentous. It is intended to make the same claim on our imagination as this act of justified rebellion, of liberation, will make in the realm of History. "When in the course of human events it becomes necessary," he writes, "for one people to dissolve the political bands which have connected them with another, and to assume among the powers of the earth, the separate and equal station to which the Laws of Nature and of Nature's God entitle them . . ."

But even he cannot have guessed, as his pen moved

on, that the words he set down next would be perhaps the most influential of the coming century, and that half a dozen of them would stand among the best known and most often quoted in the language: "We hold these truths to be sacred and undeniable, that all men are created equal, that they are endowed by their Creator with certain (inherent and) unalienable Rights, that among these are Life, Liberty and the pursuit of Happiness."[1]

Fifty years later, when all had been achieved, when the Republic was established and the Declaration had become famous as "his" contribution to a resounding moment in History, Jefferson very deliberately played down the originality of what he had written. "Neither aiming at originality of principle or sentiment," he insists, "nor yet copied from any particular and previous writing," it drew on "the harmonizing sentiments of the day, whether expressed in letters, printed essays or in the elementary books of public right, as Aristotle, Cicero, Locke, Sydney etc."[2]

Jefferson was not being modest; he was not a modest man. He was defending himself from the charge of plagiarism.

A few days before he sat down to his own draft, he had received his friend George Mason's preamble to the Virginian Constitution.[3] There he would have read: "All men are created equally free and independent and have certain inherent and natural rights . . . among which are the enjoyment of life and liberty, with the means of acquiring and possessing property, and pursuing and obtaining happiness and safety."

Nothing of this detracts from Jefferson's achievement. If anything, it enhances it.

Quite apart from the very different tone of the Declaration, which is itself a large part of what is being said, is the "bite" Jefferson achieves by reducing Mason's "the enjoyment of life and liberty, with the means of acquiring and possessing property, and pursuing and obtaining happiness and safety" to seven words only.

Gone is the Lockean reference to property and Mason's association of happiness with "safety." Set free of its link with property, Happiness, as Jefferson evokes it, moves away from its narrower sense of being *materially* fortunate towards the looser and more general one of emotional wellbeing, and assumes an importance it does not have in Mason's preamble because it stands now at the climax of a list.

"Life, Liberty and the pursuit of Happiness"— there, if we need it, is the perfect demonstration that what matters in the end is not what is thought, but the power—the clarity and bite—of what is said.

In Jefferson's formulation, without his being aware of it perhaps, something new got said. The Pursuit of Happiness is now accorded the same status, as a natural right, as Liberty and Life itself; and this is extraordinary because the three might otherwise seem to belong to separate orders of experience: Life to nature, Liberty to the social realm, Happiness—or at least the right to pursue it—to our personal and interior being. Surely this is a New World notion, an expression of American optimism and, insofar as that optimism in the next century will spread to the Old World, of American influence and the as yet unimagined future—unimagined, perhaps, but already memorably *stated*. Certainly we hear nothing of it when the French Revolution, ten years later, produces its own, equally famous trio in the Rights of Man. Liberty, Equality and Fraternity belong to a single category. They are, all three, social terms.

So what is happiness doing in the Declaration, and what does Jefferson mean by it?

Happiness is an odd word in English, so ordinary and so widely used that we seldom ask ourselves how it comes to be and to carry the wide range of emotions we associate with it. Well-being, contentment, gladness, quiet satisfaction, delight—all conditions that belong to the inner world of feeling; a sense of being at home in our own skin, at home with the world, at one with ourselves. It is a state that can be settled and continuous, but that can also be a matter of surprise, when we might think of it as joy.

But these are a set of extended meanings that have accrued to the word over time. Originally "happiness" meant something entirely material and objective, nothing at all to do with feeling.

Related to other words with the same stem, such as "happen," "happening," "happenstance," "mishap," "hapless," it meant the state of being in good standing in the world of accident and event; of being lucky, favoured by the gods and therefore pleased with what life has brought you, and it is in this earlier sense of being well-used by society and the world that happiness appears in the works of social philosophers.

That is, the two forms in which we experience "happiness"—as good luck and as the pleasure we take in it—gave rise to two separate and very different meanings of the word. And just as the opposite to good luck may be various forms of *ill*-fortune, such as indigence, ill-health, failure etc., so too there are negative states of psychological being: discontent, dissatisfaction, anxiety, nervous unrest, stress, melancholia, depression etc.

Happiness is a slide-area, difficult, unlike Life or Liberty, to define because difficult to pin down, and impossible, except within the narrow, material terms to which the seventeenth- and early eighteenth-century social philosophers limited the word, to legislate for.

Like so many of his American contemporaries, Jefferson was widely read in the English and Scottish moral and social thinkers of the previous century: the great John Locke, of course, who is essential, but also Algernon Sydney (d. 1683), author of *Discourses Concerning Government,* whom he mentions in his disclaimer as one source of "the harmonizing sentiments of the day," the Irish Francis Hutcheson (d. 1746), whose *Inquiry into Our Ideas of Beauty and Virtue* was a primary influence on Jefferson's thinking, and, most important of all in this context, Richard Cumberland, the first moral philosopher to equate the greatest good with the greatest happiness and whose "great moral principle," in his *De Legibus Naturae* of 1672, is that "the fullest, most vigorous Endeavour of each and all

Agents, in Promoting the Common Good of the rational system, contributes effectually to the Good of each Single part in such a System; under which Whole, or System, *the single individual Happiness of each, and all of us, is contained*" (my italics).

That, given its odd old-fashioned punctuation and the convoluted style of the period, is clear enough, but Cumberland makes clearer what he means by Happiness when he evokes its opposite.

"On the contrary," he tells us, "Acts opposite to such a Propensity, must produce effects opposite, and by Consequence, among many other Evils, involve us, and each of us, in Misery."

If we think of Misery as existing in such varied forms as poverty, oppression, injustice, servitude, slavery, or the sort of savagery that follows on a fall into primordial disorder, we get some idea of what Jefferson may have meant by the pursuit of happiness and why, when Mason refers to it, it is linked to "safety." It means freedom, which good government might certainly attempt to promote for the least powerful of its citizens (think of that underclass of outsiders who provides the title for Hugo's *Les Misérables*), from the worst forms of social misery: hunger, homelessness, religious or racial discrimination before the law, joblessness and the many other forms of social exclusion. But this only makes Jefferson's use of the word in the Declaration the more teasing.

Freedom from social evils is one thing, and would go some way towards making people happier, but only in the material sense and to the extent that it would relieve them of some of the conditions for *un*happiness. But Happiness, as Jefferson sets it here beside such absolute terms as Liberty and Life, seems to suggest more than this. Something larger and more uplifting, closer perhaps, among "the harmonizing sentiments of the day," to Schiller's *Freude* in the "Ode to Joy."

Whatever Jefferson's actual intentions may have been, the fact is that "the pursuit of Happiness" has always been *taken*, at least by the population at large (and where else was the Declaration finally aimed?), in its wider meaning. Not as a seventeenth-century moral philosopher might read it, as freedom from want or from intimidation by the great and powerful—a condition that can be legislated for—but as something altogether more subjective, less defined and manageable, which cannot: that sense of settled well-being of "the happy man" of long literary tradition who lives in contentment with his neighbours, the state and himself—and this was inevitable from the moment Jefferson compacted Mason's wordy formulation into a pithy seven-word phrase ("catchy" we would call it) and placed Happiness precisely where it would command maximum attention, at the climax of his trio of inalienable rights. Any possibility of its retaining its narrower socio-political meaning was overwhelmed by the surge of Jefferson's rhetoric.

What Jefferson had done, whether or not this was his intention, was to confuse, in a way that allows them to be conflated, two areas of experience that cannot really be contained within the same term—or not from a political or legislative point of view—or dealt with as one. The result is that what the Declaration appears to offer is a promise, a guarantee even, that in the polity reconceived, the republic-to-be of the United States, the right to Happiness will be a right of the same kind as the right to Life and Liberty; and this means happiness in the ordinary, everyday, subjective sense of the word, as contentment, satisfaction, pleasure—even, as the Romantic poets would soon use it, Wordsworth in one way, Blake in another, as Delight, as Joy.

In the New World, Happiness was to be a fundamental principle both of the good state, *res publica,* and of the good life that could be lived within it, and if this was not exactly what had been *promised,* it was

evoted to the manufacture of weapons of war and
he extermination, by the use of advanced technol-
gy, of several million human beings—about the
art that *techne* (art, craft, invention) has played in
r unfolding history, and where, in its late-industrial
rm as technology, it may be leading us.

In the genesis story as Protagoras tells it, Zeus, the
her of the gods, who might have seen to things
nself, passes the job of creation to the Titan Pro-
theus, and he in turn passes the actual handling
he business to his brother and twin, Epimetheus.
The brief is to distribute among the various species
pply of qualities that will provide each animal, or
ile or bird, with a life in the world that will be
ful and full, and at the same time to establish
ng them a balance that, given their difference in
strength, aggressiveness etc., and the inevitable
ry that must arise over resources, will keep the
es safe from one another and the whole system
inably intact.

imetheus begins by distributing to each of the
res in turn the special quality they will need to
t them from the elements, the fur or feathers or
hide that will keep them dry and warm; then
ngs or claws that will protect one beast from
r or the fleetness of foot, or power of flight,

from now on generally expected and would in time
be passionately pursued.

This is new within the eighteenth-century Enlightenment world and looks bravely forward to the
coming century and beyond; but it also looks boldly
back, as so much Enlightenment thinking does, to
the pre-Christian world of Greece and Rome (on Jefferson's list of previous writings that contributed to
the Declaration, Aristotle and Cicero appear equally
with Sydney and John Locke), and this too would
play its part in what was to come.

When Christianity offered its adherents happiness, it was as a reward, either for good works or for
faith, in the *next* world. The Declaration offers it as a
natural right in this one, the New World of the here
and now. The Republic, when it arrived (the Declaration, remember, was penned in 1776—the War of
Independence had still to be fought and won), would
be based on natural rights as intended by the Creator, but its external forms would mirror those of the
pagan Roman republic rather than the more recent
English one. Its elected members would form a Sen-
ate. They would sit in a Capitol. The architectural
style of its administrative centre and federal capital,
designed by Jefferson, would point to its real source
of inspiration by being neo-classical.

For all the "religious" fervour of the Declaration's rhetoric, and its conventional evocation of the Creator, the American Republic, unlike Cromwell's English one, would in spirit be secular; which is one reason why the new federation, once it was established, moved so quickly to separate Church and State.

"The Pursuit of Happiness" is the real time-bomb in the Declaration. It is also, one suspects, on Jefferson's part a language act rather than a considered political one. He was led, in the act of writing itself, to speak more radically than he knew and with another meaning than he consciously intended—though his was such a complex and divided mind that we cannot be sure of this.

Shelley called poets "the unacknowledged legislators of the world." What might better be claimed is that poets, in what they stumble upon in the business of writing itself, in the language they use and the way they deploy it, may open the way to institutional change by uncovering what, if only dimly at first, we see as a new possibility. One that, once the mind begins to work on it, becomes an actuality we cannot do without.

Unrest

In Plato's *Protagoras,* the Sophist to the dialogue offers his liste origin of things, a creation stor human life on the planet came does not claim, as Darwinism d true, or like the Biblical version sophisticated way of classical t the world as we observe it—ou history—and comes up with of the origin of all this that through what is peculiar to t one hand, and humans on t arrive at a clearer understand

Plato's interest here is in v is particularly concerned v learned, and may therefore innate, but the story Prota readings. It also has som man philosopher Heidegg tures in 1942[1]—at the pr when the entire industria or capacity to dart away underground that will allow them, when threatened, to escape. He compensates for sheer size with slowness to move, makes some animals plant-eaters only and the carnivore predators rare and with few offspring, but their prey, so that their numbers will be maintained, both fertile and abundant.

But Epimetheus, as his name tells us, has a deficiency.

Prometheus in Greek suggests forethought or thinking ahead, Epimetheus afterthought or thinking later or too late.

Epimetheus is associated, in a positive sense, with the power of memory but also with forgetting. His is the spirit of reflection. Of looking back and reconsidering, but also, as on this occasion, of oversight.

When he has distributed as wisely as possible all the qualities at his disposal, created for each creature a good and safe life and a proper balance among them, he looks around and discovers, standing patiently behind him, entirely naked and unaccommodated, another creature that he has entirely forgotten—perhaps he has left this creature till last because its needs are more difficult to satisfy than the rest. Man has been given no quality or gift and the sack is empty.

With neither feathers nor fur nor hide to protect him

from the elements, no shell to house him or cover his head, no hoof or padded foot to protect him from sharp flint or thorns, no great size to deter aggressors, no speed like the big cats to run down prey or like the mouse to scurry away, no wings to fly upward out of reach, there he stands, and there is nothing in the sack to provide for him. In desperation at this oversight, this huge error, Epimetheus turns back to Prometheus, who in his usual way takes a daring leap into the unknown and comes up with a solution.

What the gods have done for others, Man will have to do for himself. He will have to be, from start to finish, the inventor of his own nature, and to get for himself the gifts he was denied. With no *natural* advantage, he will have to become an improviser, the shaper of his world, of his environment and conditions, to the service of his own weakness. He will be a designer and builder of shelters, a maker of clothes and tools; the fashioner of the weapons he will need to keep him safe, and of the hoe and spade and plough that will force the earth to feed him; of the machines and engines at last that will give him the speed that went to the cheetah and the power of flight that went to the sparrow and the hawk. But to do all this he will need to develop in himself such "interior" and god-like qualities as the power of imagination, of invention, and these Prometheus agrees to steal for him out of the realm of the gods, from Heaven itself; beginning with the earliest and most essential of skills, and the source of all technology, the knowledge of how to make fire and carry it with him wherever he goes.

This version of the creation myth sets Man in a heroic light. His life is endless unaided struggle against the odds. Everything that has to do with him, everything human, beginning from an original error, an oversight on the part of the Creator, will be an attempt to rectify that error and make good what was denied him, to turn what was an essential weakness to strength. He is to be the self-sufficient custodian and creator of his own nature, his own history and fate.

A lonely figure, heroic but also restlessly anxious and eternally incomplete, this is Man the Maker, whose peculiar gift is craft or *techne,* the capacity to forge, shape, fashion; to take a world that had no place for him and make it his own. To turn wilderness into a fruitful landscape and lay down roads to move on; above all, to found societies and build cities, those ideal human artefacts, the embodiment of neighbourliness and civic virtue and industry, of good governance and the rule of law.

But the special quality with which Man is endowed

in this version of our story, and with which, in a risky experiment, he has been sent forth to claim the world—this *techne* and capacity for invention—implies other and earlier qualities. Curiosity, for example, and, preliminary even to that, a flair for observation, for seeing below the surface and beyond the recording of singular phenomena, for setting two separate things side by side and deducing a relationship; the capacity for productive thought. A capacity, simply, for looking about and being puzzled and asking why, and moving on from puzzlement to the demand for an answer. And what this speaks of is dissatisfaction, a sense of insecurity and final incompleteness; a belief always that there is more to be discovered and claimed, and that until you have grasped this "more," and have it in hand, you will be neither happy nor whole.

What Plato uncovers, at least in Heidegger's late and "modern" reading of the *Protagoras,* is what it is in the make-up of our human nature, our psychology, our *psyche* or soul, that makes Man supremely, among the creatures, the one that sets out to take the world he is in and shape it to his needs, but more significantly, to be led, by the spirit of invention, beyond the mere satisfaction of those needs to what, already in Plato's time, was the wonder of "civilisation," the complex working unit of the city-state; "Athens," with its dedication to order, productivity, democracy and the rule of law, to science, the arts of sculpture and architecture, of poetry, music, drama, dance, games and the sort of mind-activity that is represented by the schools of philosophical enquiry of which Plato's Academy is just one.

What Protagoras identifies as the irritant in human nature that makes the pearl is our essential restlessness, our *dis*satisfaction, our *un*rest; a *lack* in us that has endlessly to be filled. But this "endlessly" is also the cause, in the individual, of a spiritual disabling that it is the role of philosophy and the rival Athenian schools, in their different ways, to cure.

I will return to the philosophical schools, and their versions of the "talking cure," in just a moment. What I want to look at now is another creation story, one that springs this time from the other side of our heritage, the Judeo-Christian, though this too, like the Epimetheus version, is not the usual one. It comes in a poem, "The Pulley," by the seventeenth-century devotional poet George Herbert:[2]

> When God at first made man,
> Having a glass of blessings standing by;
> "Let us" (said He) "pour on him all we can:
> Let the world's riches, which dispersèd lie,
>   Contract into a span."

So strength first made a way;
Then beauty flowed, then wisdom, honour, pleasure:
When almost all was out, God made a stay,
Perceiving that alone of all His treasure
    Rest in the bottom lay.

"For if I should" (said He)
"Bestow this jewel also on my creature,
He would adore my gifts instead of me,
And rest in Nature, not the God of Nature:
    So both should losers be.

"Yet let him keep the rest,
But keep them with repining restlessness:
Let him be rich and weary, that at least,
If goodness lead him not, yet weariness
    May toss him to my breast."

Here, as in the Epimetheus story, the Creator has gifts to distribute but decides, deliberately, to withhold the last of them. Man, he tells us in a nice pun, can have the rest, but the gift of "rest" itself—peace, contentment, final satisfaction—will be denied him. Unrest will be his condition until he finds rest in the Lord.

Though these readings of Man's nature, of where, as humans, we stand in the crowded ranks of creation, belong to cultures—Greek and Christian—that are often seen as opposite and antagonistic, they

ent, is the reversal that has occurred in our notion of "unrest" in a century of iPods, mobile phones, multitasking; of YouTube, Facebook, Twitter; of news bites, 24-hour news cycles, jump-cut video clips; and the stimulation of our senses at every moment, in public as well as private spaces, by verbal admonitions and warnings and visual enticements of every sort, from rolling advertisements at bus stops and TV monitors at supermarket check-outs, to plasma screens in bars and pubs.

Far from being an existential state of anxiety requiring cure, unrest is itself the cure, and for something quite opposite but equally close and pervasive: the fear of inactivity, of stillness; most of all, of the withdrawal of every form of chatter or noise in an extended and unendurable *silence.*

As if that terror of "the eternal silence of infinite spaces" that haunted Pascal in the seventeenth century had found its new form on Earth, and had now to be exorcised from every lift in every public building; every bar and restaurant (right down to the toilets); every supermarket or boutique or waiting room in every city, great or small, of the civilised world; even from our telephones as we wait to be "connected." But then it was Pascal who first identified in us an earlier and more essential anxiety. "I have discovered," he tells us, "that all our ills derive from a single cause. That we cannot live at peace in a *room*."[3] (So much for Montaigne's "little back-shop" and the consolations of retirement into the self.)

A lone figure in a closed and lonely room is our image now for existential dread. That inner life where, for Montaigne as for the ancients, the freedom of self-containment, of self-sufficiency was to be worked for and found, is no longer a choice because it is no longer an option.

Imagine a modern politician who is announcing his retirement telling the media pack at a press conference, "I'm hoping to spend more time with myself." A Montaigne or a Jefferson might get away with it, but a Bill Clinton or a Tony Blair would be mocked around the clock from Wapping to Waterloo or Woolloomooloo. The "little back-shop all our own" is to be escaped at all cost, by more and more adventuring elsewhere—on the moon, in the furthest reaches of space—or is to be filled with noise and such activity, virtual or real, as is permanently available at the touch of a keyboard.

It would be easy to dismiss this as shallow, mindless; to see in the sensory overload of these contemporary diversions a sign—like consumerism and the pursuit of the fifteen minutes of celebrity we have all been promised—of the decadence that comes with affluence, and the fact that we now have on our hands so much time that has to be filled. But there is another and more interesting possibility.

It is that this is a new form of "being" in which the Ego is by-passed not in the old way, by contemplation in the Greek and Roman sense of internal argument, or in the Eastern way through meditation—both of which require and make a virtue of silence—but through an overload that is the equivalent, in mental activity, of those extreme forms of physical activity that are a feature of some sports. We know that the high levels of endorphins released by intensive physical exercise produce euphoria. Perhaps the exercise of the brain, when it is involved in dealing with rapid stimulus and response, as in video games or in the sort of attention we call upon when we are multi-tasking, creates in us a similar rush of well-being, of exhilaration, elation; an awareness of intense personal presence, in a fast-moving and richly crowded world that we are intensely in tune with, and where a new form of "happiness" may be found.

What this suggests is the possibility that the mind—or, more precisely these days, the brain—is still evolving, and at an increasing rate as technology presents it with new forms to master and new stimuli to respond to. This would mean that the mind, as Aristotle might have known it, and Montaigne too in the state of slow change that existed in the long period between his century and the fourth century BC, is quite a different mind from the one a five-year-old is employing when he deals with a video game today.

One aspect of the Epimetheus version of the creation story is that in this account of things the history of Man can have no end, is never done. So long as we are driven by the need to make up for our needs; by the restless sense that we are not yet fully assured of our place in the world and our hold on its swarming phenomena; so long as there is more to be discovered and made, more to grasp for and make real, we must go on inventing ourselves. And as technology goes on increasing, and at greater speed, so the agency in us that allows us to deal with the world must go on evolving to keep up with it. Jefferson's guarantee of happiness for all might be seen, in this context, to have been made to a generation of beings that had still to come into full existence, to be a condition that was to be aimed for rather than an immediately available gift.

It was Jefferson's contemporary, the Frenchman

Marie Jean Antoine Nicolas de Caritat, Marquis de Condorcet, who first understood the power of this idea of "futurity" and in 1793, in his *Sketch for a Historical Picture of the Progress of the Human Mind,* laid out a theory of "History as Progress." It would be hard to exaggerate the importance of this astonishing work.

First published, after Condorcet's death, in 1795, it replaced forever what had till then been an unchallenged orthodoxy: that history was a closed system, a storehouse of *exempla;* of human character-types, events, movements that were fixed in number and endlessly repeatable from age to age, so that for every apparently new event, or great man or "change," there was an existing prototype or model. Condorcet's idea of Progress was one of those Copernican moments when a reality, as we had previously taken it to be, was turned on its head.

Condorcet considers the progress of Man through nine stages, from the nomadic hordes of pre-history to his own early-Industrial present and the establishment, in 1789, of the French Republic. He concludes that "from observation of the progress which science and civilisation have hitherto made, and from the analysis of the march of human understanding and the development of his faculties, Nature has fixed no limits to our hopes . . . The advantages that must result from this state of improvement . . . can have no limit but the absolute perfection of the human species."[4]

Such new orientations in thinking produce others, and rapidly. The notion that history might be progressive rather than cyclical, that an event, a thought, an individual man (Napoleon, for example) might have no precedent—might, in the whole of time as we knew it, never have occurred or been seen before, and was original rather than recurrent—directed our attention away from the past and towards the future. We no longer had to look to the past for the interpretation of present happenings, or to consult it, study its events and types, so that when they arrived in a new guise we could recognise and identify them. Our attention had now to be used in a new way, in developing an eye for occurrence rather than recurrence, for the unknown, the unexpected, the unlikely, the entirely new. Time had another shape and we stood at a different point in its unfolding. Once the future had been opened up to our vision as the direction in which we might turn our face, it developed a vastness as infinite, if only in prospect, in our imagination, as the immemorial past. All kinds of new ideas would depend upon it: Darwin's theory of evolution, when it came half a century later; in the arts the notion of an *avant-garde*—that only what had never been done before, what moved things forward, what belonged, like Wagner's "Music of the Future," to Progress and the New, could be properly significant.

The eighteenth-century belief in a progressive future, the assurance of an improved and better time to come, together with a growing sense, as I suggested earlier, that true goodness is the goodness that we extend to others (as Condorcet puts it in the last part of the *Sketch,* "the general welfare of the species, of the society in which one lives"), accounts for a new willingness in men and women to devote themselves, politically, but now with an almost religious fervour, to the future; to living so that future generations may be "happy" even if *they* are not. This is the note we hear, of such plangency and with such a mixture of hopeless desperation and hope, in Chekhov's sad comedies of Russian life at the turn of the twentieth century: in the doctor, Astrov, in *Uncle Vanya,* and Vershinin in *The Three Sisters.*

"I wondered," Astrov tells the old nurse Marya, "whether the people who come after us, in a hundred years' time, the people for whom we are now blasting a trail—will they remember us kindly?" Later in the play, he comes back to the idea, but more bitterly: "The people who come a hundred years, or a couple of hundred years, after us and despise us for having lived in so stupid and hopeless a fashion—perhaps they'll find a way to be happy."

Vershinin is in no doubt of it, nor of the part he must play in bringing it about: "All the same, I think I do know one thing which is not only true but also very important. I'm sure of it—oh, if only I could convince you that there's not going to be any happiness for our own generation . . . We've just got to work and work. All happiness is reserved for our descendants, our remote descendants."

Chekhov is wonderfully sympathetic towards these good men with their passionate feeling for others and their yearning—their sentimental nostalgia we might call it—for a future that will justify their existence as they cannot justify it in the present, even to themselves. He recognises their pain, their desperate sense of being, as Dostoevsky puts it, ciphers, superfluous, unnecessary men. But their rush to self-denial and self-sacrifice disturbs him.

What haunts us in the plays is that the future for which these characters are so ready to sacrifice their lives and their own chance of happiness has already arrived now and passed. We know only too well the fate of that future generation—Shukhov, for example, where we found him in his Gulag—who will be the inheritors of those "happy lives." Behind Condorcet's optimistic belief in infinite progress we hear Mao's proclamation of "perpetual revolution" and the murderous slogans of the Cultural Revolution, Trotsky's scornful evocation of the "scrapheap of history" that is reserved for those who stand in the way of historical necessity; and on the other side of politics, what was put to idealistic young SS men after Heydrich's announcement to the Wannsee Conference, in 1942, of the Final Solution: that whatever the moral cost to those whose duty it would be to dispose of the millions who could have no place in it, future generations of the Thousand Year Reich would recognise their sacrifice and, as Astrov puts it, remember them kindly.

Condorcet was a mathematician—his special interest was probability theory—but also a philosopher with a keen interest in education (he designed the education system that would later be used throughout post-Revolutionary France). He was also a member of the National Assembly in the best days of the Revolution, a moderate who voted against the execution of the king. Hounded out by the Jacobins, he wrote his *Sketch* on the run, and died, by poison perhaps, in hiding, five months before Thermidor. He had a large influence on the thinkers, and especially the poets, of the generation immediately behind him: Wordsworth, Coleridge, de

Quincy, who wrote *The Confessions of an English Opium Eater,* the Ettrick Shepherd James Hogg, who wrote *The Private Memoirs and Confessions of a Justified Sinner,* Novalis and Hölderlin in Germany—all born around 1770—who, as they came into their twenties, found his idea of infinite energy, of perpetual change and progress, of particular significance to their own rising wave of revolutionary Romanticism.

They were the first generation—there have been many since—to recognise energetic unrest as a requisite of creative genius and to cultivate intensity for its own sake as a reassurance of presence, of being, though the intensity was not always of a happy kind, and did not, for their purposes, need to be. As well as Joy, Delight, Ecstasy, there was also Terror, the source of the Sublime, and intensity could sometimes manifest itself as Dejection (Depression we would call it) or Rage. Their chief demand was that it should be permanent, that the emotions should at all times be at the highest pitch, and, when this could not be achieved (that is, when the body lapsed into the ordinary), it had to be maintained, as we see in Coleridge's case, and de Quincy's, with drugs. The "fine frenzy" to which these poets aspired could also be a form of madness.

For Condorcet, as for the Plato-Protagoras of the

Epimetheus story, Man is driven; there is no end to what he cannot become. The need to discover and invent, to remake, improve, is essential to him. He must pursue perfection come what may. More land must be brought under cultivation, with higher productivity per acre; higher production, higher sales, more profits must be our goal; a higher population to make up the workforce and the pool of consumers, a higher leaving age for school students, a higher life expectancy. Only when all these, as Condorcet lays them out in the tenth part of the *Sketch,* have been achieved at last, and perfection is within his grasp, will Man be happy.

It is no coincidence that Condorcet's close contemporary was Goethe. There is something Faustian in this new, this "modern" version of Man as both the happy child of progress, of the will to knowledge and power, and its endlessly unresting slave.

Happiness in the Flesh

One of the most striking features of twenty-first century living, in what we think of as our part of the world, is the return of the body as our most immediate, and in some cases our only, assurance of presence, of the rich and crowded and actively happening world-we-are-in.

The body has become natural again, and essentially good. It is subject to decay, of course, and eventually to death, but for most of us it is a source of innocent pleasure and happiness, of joy in the flesh, and increasingly for some of a kind of worship in which, as I shall want to suggest later, it has largely replaced what in earlier times would have been called the Self. This is only to say that for a large number of people these days the material or physical world is more important than the inner life. The body is what most completely represents them, even to themselves. If we no longer see it as fallen or corrupt, it is because we no longer see nature that way, and it is to nature that it belongs.

This is both a new and a very old view of the body.

It has its roots in that part of our culture that derives from the classical world, and is one of the things that were revived and returned to us with what we call the Renaissance.

For the Greeks and Romans, the human body was an animal body. Clearly, humanity, endowed as it is with reason, speech, a capacity for inventing and making, and for social organisation of a most complex kind, stands at the top of the animal ladder; but as in other world views—Hinduism, Buddhism, for example—the separation between the species was not absolute. In classical mythology, girls could be turned, on the whim of the gods, into birds, like Philomela the nightingale, or trees or plants, like Daphne the laurel, the reed Syrinx, Clytie the sunflower, or even into a bear, like Callisto. Zeus, in his role as lover, could take the form of an eagle, a bull, a swan; young men, after death, return as flowers (Hyacinthus, Narcissus) or become constellations like the twins (Gemini) Castor and Pollux.

This fluidity of forms is what animates Ovid's book of "changes," the *Metamorphoses*. In the medium of words, as virtuosic syntactical act and visual event, he made the emergence of one life out of another, the melting before our eyes of girlish sinuosity into the flow of water, the breaking of limbs into branches and leaves, so convincing in their actuality as to be "real," and if ordinary men and women did not believe in them as *fact*—belief in our sense of the word was not required—they did recognise that what these "fables" pointed to was a larger and more general truth. That all of creation was connected, and shared the same life-energy; was part of a continuity. That the world, *this* world, was whole and "good." Animals, including humans, were innocent. The pleasures of the body were also innocent, a source of happiness and ease. Sensual delight was a gift of the gods that was meant to be celebrated, and whose celebration, in games, in dance, in eating and drinking, in love-making, was its own way of showing gratitude for the gift.

What the classical moralists recommended was moderation—as a guarantee of psychological balance as well as good health—*nec nimis* (nothing in excess) is the phrase that Horace, who has a supreme gift for such concise and memorable formulations, has passed down to us; but they did not think of carnal pleasure as sinful or as a reason for shame.

The body was not holy—a temple as the Church would later call it—to be preserved from unhallowed use; it was meant to be used—that is, enjoyed. If the sexual life involved distress or evil, this had nothing to do with the sinfulness of the flesh, but with such psychological factors as jealousy, loss of self-containment and control, the pain of rejection or betrayal and the shaming anger and self-disgust that may follow upon them—all these the human consequences of the war between the sexes as Catullus and others report upon it, writing in, from its battle-zones and skirmishes, with personal accounts of triumph or of humiliation and defeat.

Carnal pleasure, which involves and interests us all, is one of the major subjects of classical writing from Sappho and the poets of the Greek Anthology to a long line of Latin poets: Catullus, Horace, Propertius, Ovid. Ovid especially has a sensibility so "modern," so contemporary to all times, that he has been a living voice in every period from Ronsard and Donne to Frank O'Hara in our own.

His *Ars Amatoria*, a cheeky exercise in youthful exhibitionism and the pursuit of sexual adventure in the big city, is the work of a young man-about-town (a *persona,* in fact: Ovid when he wrote it was nearly fifty) who delights in every form of doubtful behaviour, rejects every respectable career that might be available to a Roman of his class, and, as opportunistic seducer, sometime lover, hero not of the battlefield or the law courts but of the bedchamber and bed, devotes the whole range of his energy and interest to the pleasures of the flesh.[1]

This is the classical work that poets and writers throughout Europe in the sixteenth century turn back to as their textbook and guide to a freer form of living, and the rediscovery of the body as a new world of pleasure and happiness.

Pietro Aretino in Italy produces a suite of sonnets, the *Sonetti Lussuriosi* (Lascivious Sonnets), that break with the Petrarchan tradition of idealised love in poems that are frankly and provocatively carnal—and which he takes to a point that even now seems close to the limits of the permissible.[2]

In France, Rabelais sets up, in his Abbey of Thélème, a parody religious order whose only rule is *Fay çe que vouldras* (Do what thou wilt), an institution devoted to the breaking of all taboos and the restoration of the flesh as a source of riotous but harmless and joyful misrule.

Half a century later, Ovid provides the model again for the stance that John Donne adopts, and the voice he uses, to challenge convention, defy authority and claim his own place in the world as nothing less, or more, than poet and lover. The scramble for office—in law, in the army, at court—he leaves to what he scornfully calls "countrey ants."[3] An early member of his own Me Generation, he makes a grand rejection of all social ties, all ties to nation or polity, in favour of a community that consists solely of his mistress and himself: "She is all States, and all Princes I, Nothing else is."[4] He even challenges the centrality of the sun (that newish scientific concept), which he now harnesses to their private universe and use:

> Thou sunne art half as happy as we,
>   In that the world's contracted thus . . .
> Shine here to us, and thou art every where;
> This bed thy centre is, these walls, thy spheare.

His celebration of his mistress's body is free, happy, entirely without shame or guilt, and expresses itself in language so active and sensual that it not only reproduces, as far as language can, his own energy and excitement, but attempts to transfer that energy, with its kinetic rhythms, to us as we read:

> Licence my roving hands, and let them go
> Behind, before, above, between, below . . .
> Oh my America, my new found land.

The body has always been a source of joy of the kind Donne is expressing, and if there were those, during the long period when Christianity and its teachings held sway in Europe, for whom it was guilty joy, shameful, even degrading, there must have been many who felt nothing of this: felt, that is, as Donne did and held their tongue about it. Sexual joy is too overwhelmingly physical to be ignored. Such sceptics, or secret heretics, must have decided that the Church Fathers were somehow wrong about the body, and that their parish priests were either equally wrong or liars; or that they themselves were somehow lost but happy about it, or lost and not.

Certainly there were times and places, among the Cathars, for example, in south-western France in the thirteenth century, where sexual energy and the open expression of it could not be contained and broke out as revolt. And of course there were other parts of the world, equally religious, where sexual energy and its joyful expression were not incompatible with a sense of the sacred or the practice of faith. The temples of India, with their exuberant facades where sculptured figures rejoice in voluptuous poses and engagements of every kind, are monuments to the sacredness of the flesh, and to moments of carnal and spiritual union.

The frank expression of sexual happiness in a poem, in words, is one thing. Painting and the depiction of sensual joy in paint—despite Horace's famous phrase that links poetry and painting as sister arts—is something quite other.

Though flat and two-dimensional, painting tricks the eye into perceiving a third, creating depth and distance where there is none, giving a bare arm or leg a roundness it does not have, but also a softness, since the visual is not the only sense that painting appeals to and plays with. Objects it picks out on the flat surface of a canvas or a plaster wall have textures we feel we could reach out and test between our fingers. Flesh, and the blood that gives it colour, has a palpable warmth, but the shadow it throws is cool. No painter better controls these effects, or deploys them more richly, than the Flemish artist Peter Paul Rubens.

Almost exactly Donne's contemporary, Rubens—already, at sixty, by the standards of his time an old man (Shakespeare was dead at fifty-two)—sets out to paint his second wife, Helena Fourment. The painting still has the power, even in our own century, to shock.

Caught bare-footed and naked in a room with a crimson carpet and a crimson cushion at her feet, she has snatched up a black fur cape with a gold border to cover herself, but this spur-of-the-moment act only serves to emphasise her nudity: bare feet and legs, bare shoulders, the cape caught up below her belly so that she has to use her arms in an inadequate, endearingly awkward way to cover her breasts. She seems younger than her twenty-four years. Perhaps Rubens was thinking of her as she was when he married her, his sixteen-year-old bride.[5]

It is a "corridor" moment, an after-dark household moment to which only her husband might be privy, or should be. Instead he paints it to express and share—but with whom, we wonder—the immense joy he finds in her presence: her being, her youth, her glowing beauty, her flesh; and to confess—again, to whom?—how happy they are in their togetherness in the flesh. The gratitude he feels is part of the offering. He is showing, in the surest way that is possible to him, in paint, the privilege he feels in her having given herself to him.

All this is so intensely private, sacred perhaps, that we are astonished that the painting is there to be seen. We know that Rubens regarded it as a personal possession, a precious record of their intimate life together; he names it, *Het Pelsken*, in his will, and leaves it to her.

But paintings are *made* to be seen. There is something here that Rubens wanted revealed, and in such

alled upon to set her child aside for a
rip and, as directed, raising an arm here,
er neck there, shifting her weight from
t to the right, strike a pose as Callisto or
a or Flora, or as a close, convenient servant-
d companion (only much later a wife) take
e of Bathsheba or A Woman Bathing.

vorld these Northern painters work in is
d in the domestic but moves easily from the
to the theatrical, and from contemporary
ts to the remote mythological past. In a way
ems essentially Baroque, the cluttered rooms
e interiors, with so many props close at hand,
t the back-stage "tyring rooms" of a private
e where someone is always undressing or dress-
.

it happens that in the Rembrandt double por-
we cannot be quite sure what it is we have got. It
be the illustration of a parable, the exposure—
, in that case, a deal of good-natured sympathy—
outhful debauchery, though that is not the message
take from its cheerful exuberance.

What it clearly is, whatever the "subject," is the pic-
re of a couple, caught here in a private moment but not
all disconcerted by our intrusion.

He, elaborately decked out as a cavalier, with a

Peter Paul Rubens, *Het Pelsken*
(*Hélène Fourment in a Fur Wrap*), c. 1630s,
Kunst-historisches Museum, Vienna.

a way that it would be powerfully clear. It is something not only about the woman, the girl, his wife Helena Fourment, about the way he sees her and the sensual response she wakes in him, which is everywhere in the painting. It is his own brimming happiness that he wants to show.

Three years earlier, Rubens' younger contemporary Rembrandt had produced a famous double portrait, if that is what it is, of himself and his young wife, Saskia. The painting, where it hangs now in the Gemäldegalerie in Dresden, is called *The Prodigal Son with a Whore.*

Rubens and Rembrandt both work as Northern painters often do, close to home. Household and studio are sometimes one. We know the interior of these Flemish and Dutch houses from the paintings: closed, half-dark, stocked with heavy furniture, crowded with objects of every sort—oriental carpets, furs, brocaded silks, satins, leather, old pieces of armour, glazed pitchers, metal ewers—that can be glimpsed, from one painting to the next, as background decoration in domestic portraits and genre pictures, or as "props" in a mythological set-piece.

We also recognise the painters' wives, as a young

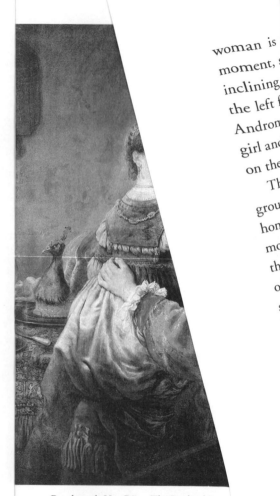

Rembrandt Van Rijn, *The Prodigal Son w*
with Saskia), c. 1635, Gemäldega

sword at his waist and a glowing feather in his hat, looks back over his shoulder, sees us and bursts out laughing. (How often in these Northern pictures people laugh outright—an expression of excessive emotion too undignified and naturalistic, too distorting of the ideal, for Italian painting.)

She too, made aware perhaps by his burst of laughter that we have come upon them, turns and meets our gaze; we have caught her seated on his knee. She is demure but dignified. Confident. Preparing to smile. They are on their way to bed, but show no sign of embarrassment; he raises his long glass and toasts us. Held high, it resembles a lamp that floods with light her face, her neck, the gold chain she is wearing, the shallow scoop of white lawn below the collar of her gown, his snowy feather, his left hand on the gleaming folds of her skirt.

What the man, who is clearly the painter, seems to be celebrating and to be inviting us, since we have so unexpectedly appeared, to witness, is a moment of domestic bliss, of conjugal felicity. Perhaps the dressing-up part of it is a piece of private theatre, the acting out of a sexual fantasy, titillating foreplay. If it is, that too he is willing to show without embarrassment and to share.

What he is also sharing with us is the ordinary

richness of the world, its press of objects, some of them useful in an ordinary way, some of them both that and props to be taken up and given a new use and significance in the theatre of happy play: all of them—fringed cushion, oriental rug, gold chain, silk skirt, glass, brocaded curtain, feather, sword-hilt, glowing flesh—brush-stroked in, since he is after all Rembrandt the painter, with the greatest possible appeal to the senses in their varied textures and the play of light upon them, in the utter joy, one would want to say, that he finds in all this as artist and technician. Not simply in the moment, and in the two human participants and what they are making for, but in his being-in-the-world, and in all these objects that he has so lovingly rendered.

Amsterdam and Antwerp at this moment, like Venice just decades before, are great trading centres. Objects—commodities—matter. Making them visually actual, in brushstrokes on canvas, is the artist's way of dealing with what merchants handle in the world of affairs: a feeling for materiality—the texture, weight, colour, of cloth or fur or metal, but also of such exotic blooms as peonies and tulips, the iridescent plumage of partridge and peacock, the rind of melons and pomegranates. The bringing alive of all this in paint is another form of the same energy that goes, elsewhere, into adventuring and trading out there in the Caribbean or the Indies, and can be made visible in the domestic world of a couple, the painter *en zijn huysvroouw*, on their way to bed. Part of that energy is sexual. It is a close step, as Donne shows, from the adventuring of "behind, before, above, between, below" to "Oh my America, my new found land."

Perhaps the closest we get in painting to the bold and joyful sensuality of Donne's poem is in Rubens' extraordinary image of Helena Fourment. What it reaches for is a moment of spontaneous appearance that seems too fleeting for paint—for the painstaking business of preparing the canvas, making a sketch, mixing the paints, getting the model to hold her pose. Rubens here is reproducing what struck his senses in the instant when the image of this woman flashed on his eye. What the picture anticipates is the candid camera-flash, a figure caught in bright light as she steps out of the dark.

Rubens, of course, is the master in his period, the Baroque, of the large-scale historical painting that is all drama, spectacle, dynamic action and energy. These vast works came in dozens from the Rubens workshop, Biblical or mythological scenes, allegorical set-pieces, contemporary events—the cycle he painted, for example, for Marie de Medici in France—in which, given all the paraphernalia, and bravura and dash of Rubens' "theatre," the political is raised to the status of myth and endowed with "divine" authority. He produced these compositions to order, employing an astonishing flair for dramatic gesture, and drawing on his memory, which was vast and encyclopedic, for poses from the classical repertoire or the modern Italian masters that he could, in each case, shape to his own occasion and play with in such a way that they both recalled the past, and his creative continuity with it, and at the same time displayed his individual boldness and originality; and when it came to convincing background detail for this period or that, the Biblical, or the classical world of Greece or Rome, there was again his encyclopedic memory to call upon for antiquarian accuracy.

Skilled workmen executed what Rubens had designed and he added the finishing touches: the adjustment of a pose, a dash of colour no assistant would dare aspire to, individual brushstrokes. His genius was essential to these works, but the question remains of how "authentic" they are, how much they are his. The eye and the mind are his but not the hand. Which is why we put such a high value on the bravura sketches, which are so full of the immediate energy of conception and so characteristic in the boldness of their lines and washes (as executed they are small, but already gigantic in their dynamic power, in the scope of what they have imagined) but also on the late landscapes, which we know were so personally dear to him, and the domestic images of Helena and her children (the last of whom, a girl, was born eight months after Rubens' death).

What makes a "private" work like *Het Pelsken* so precious, and rare at this late point in Rubens' career, is that we know that it is his hand, and the energy of his mind and body, that produced every brushstroke. The painting is the product not just of his vision, his powers of composition, but of his *presence,* as we know him—the man himself—from other more public occasions.[6]

Wordsworth defined the making of poetry as "emotion recollected in tranquility."[7] The poet makes the emotion he creates real to us *now,* but to him it belongs to experience that has to be called up out of the past and re-collected. What he needs for the making of it now is a quiet moment when he can be still, and, by reflecting, relive what he felt as words.

Het Pelsken is nothing like that. Painting is a physical act in which the painter's energy is dynamically of the moment, in the quickness of his eye, the sureness of his hand, as brushstrokes and paint reproduce what he feels in the moment itself. That energy is a form of joy. What he is setting down, direct onto the canvas, is his happiness, and this, perhaps, is as close as we will ever get to it, to another man's being; the closest we will get—and we take the phrase in both senses—to happiness in the flesh.

The Way We Live Now

Ask any one of your friends or neighbours if they are happy and the answer they will probably give is that they have nothing to complain of.

What they mean is that the good life as previous generations might have conceived it has been attained. Medical science ensures that fewer children die in infancy, that most infectious diseases have been brought under control and the worst of them—smallpox, plague, TB, polio—have in most parts of the world been eliminated; that except for a few areas in Africa famine is no longer known among us; that in advanced societies like our own we are cared for by the state from cradle to grave.

We do complain, of course, but our complaints are trivial, mostly ritual. Our politicians lack vision, interest rates are too high, the pace of modern living is too hectic; the young have no sense of duty, family values are in decline. The good life, it seems, is not enough. We have nothing to complain of, we are "happy enough"; but we are not *quite* happy. We are still, somehow, unsatisfied, and this dissatisfaction, however vaguely conceived, is deeply felt.

If pressed, our friends or neighbours will probably tell us that what they are suffering from is "stress"; a sense, again vaguely conceived, that in the world about them, as they feel it and as it touches their lives, all is not well. They do not, in the end, feel secure or safe.

This dissatisfaction, this lack of a final assurance of safety, is our later version of what the *Protagoras* identified as "unrest." But what is it, in a society where so many of the conditions that might once have stood in the way of happiness have been removed or brought under control, that makes us so uneasy, so fearful that our lives are not yet safely in hand, that the future we are facing—and this preoccupation with the future, which is itself relatively new, is surely part of it—may be darker than such optimists as Condorcet believed? That the world as we now see it is too large, and the forces within it that govern our lives are too remote, too complex to grapple with?

For most of human history, the world as we had direct experience of it extended little further than an hour's walk would take us in any direction from where we lived, which was also, in most cases, where we were born.

Only the rich, who might have a country estate as well as a house in town, would travel further: half a day or so on horseback, later by coach. Or magistrates on their way to quarterly assizes. Or pedlars, or men and women on pilgrimage, or soldiers and sailors who went to foreign places and brought back stories of "Cannibals that each other eat / The Anthropophagi, and men whose heads / Do grow beneath their shoulders."

For the majority, the world beyond their immediate view barely existed for them. If it was a source of anxiety it was through old memories of invasion, or the arrival among them, fearful because entirely unpredictable, of the first signs on the body of plague.

Space, like almost everything, was measured in terms of the body which was the measure of all: "as far as the eye can see," "a handspan," "rule of thumb," "a hundred paces."

Soil, local weather patterns, seasonal fruits and harvests, the time for shooting birds or hunting wild boar, for gathering mushrooms or kindling—these were the conditions that made space, but also time, conceivable.

Only at rare moments in history, when a city-state

or nation acquired colonies—Rome after 100 BC, Britain, Spain, France, Portugal, Holland in modern times—did ordinary men and women have a sense of being connected to something more than the few streets of the town or village they had grown up in: through a son who was serving overseas, a neighbour who had emigrated or a business connection; or, in the households of the well-to-do, through what came to the table from places that might be weeks or even months away: tomatoes, pineapples, exotic spices.

All this is very different from the world as we see it now. The bit of it we deal with at first hand and move in daily (unless we are commuters) may be no larger than it ever was; but our consciousness of where we stand has enormously expanded.

What we inhabit now is the Planet. What we see ourselves as being part of, and each in our small way responsible for, is something even larger than that, an abstraction, but one that burns and rages all around us: *Die Umwelt*, as the Germans call it, *L'Ambiente* in Italian, in English the Environment—a word that even fifty years ago would have been, in its present sense, puzzling, even meaningless, and is now among the commonest in daily speech.

Ever since it was established in the sixteenth century that the Earth was not flat, we have seen it in our mind's eye, with its familiar oceans and continents, as "the globe." Slightly askew on its axis, this was the form in which we peered down at its capes and bays on schoolroom models and set it spinning under our hand.

Then early in the 1970s a point was reached, far out in space, from which it could at last be filmed and beamed back to us; so that we could, in the same instant, be here in our regular place on its surface and at the same time observe it, small, round, lonely-looking, out there in its far-off planetary life, as for centuries, in all its coolness and distance, we had observed that other close heavenly body, the moon.

The effect was eerie. There it was, absorbed in its own purely mechanical business of swimming through space, and here we were, actually on it but at the same time seeing it as apart from us, remote and other. From that moment the universe as it existed in our consciousness took a new form; our lives developed new dimensions. So did the planet.

We felt a new sort of wonder at the series of astonishing accidents that must have occurred to create the piled-up mountain ranges of its landmasses, produce just the atmosphere that was needed to support such a teeming variety of mineral and plant and animal life, the sea creatures and land creatures, one of which—another product of that series of accidents—was *us*. Us with our curious needs and capacities and desires, our complex nervous system and brain, our individual quirks and tics and habits.

One of the things that was suddenly clear, now that we saw the planet small and whole, was what a unique and complex system it was, and how closed. That as creatures we were all in the same boat; that from the point of view of the planet itself, this ball of matter that was pursuing its own course through space and time, we might be of only passing interest. For all our billions, and for all we had done and made over the centuries, we were at this distance invisible.

The experience made us too feel small. This was Earth, which had seemed so vast in our slowly acquired knowledge and exploration of it, and so close in our daily experience of its light and dark, its warm and cool, its grassy greens and sky blues; yet how small and unsupported-looking it was out there. And everything around us that we had for so long taken for granted—trees, clouds, seas, birds, insects, the cities we live in, the container ships, the planes—depended on the accidental balance it had hit upon—

who knows when?—and maintained over millions of years, but which, in whatever future it had out there, might be so fragile. That was the new vision.

When Dostoevsky's Kirillov in *The Demons* considered the Earth, what he was touched by was "a little green leaf, yellow at the edge," which was his assurance that life, and the Earth, would go on without him. What we are touched by now, with a mixture of pathos and concern, is the planet itself; its wholeness, the interdependency of its creatures down to the smallest and most rare—a yellow-bellied tree-frog in the Amazon, a marsupial mouse—and the fragility of their healthy continuance.

This was the beginning of a new sensibility. It took in the small, but it also saw things in global terms: a global Environment—weather patterns like El Niño and La Niña, greenhouse gases, the connection across vast tracts of the Earth between small happenings (the Butterfly Effect) and larger ones that might be registered thousands of miles away; global Security, global Culture, and in an age of large-scale management, the global Economy with its Market Forces, its International Trading Agreements, the IMF, the World Bank—a global power with its own mystique and the authority to demand instant obedience and absolute belief. By the time of the Global Financial Crisis towards the end of the first decade of the new century, the Global Economy had become our contemporary equivalent of what we had once stood in awe of, and fearfully but hopelessly propitiated, under the name of Fate or the Gods.

What the classical schools offered their adherents was the removal from their lives of the uncontrolled, their vulnerability to what was "external"—external, that is, to the Self: dependency on others, fear of Fate or the Gods, fear of death. Happiness lay in self-containment, self-sufficiency. The one thing that none of the schools doubted was the importance of the Self as the purest agency of being and its need to be protected from the distractions, the temptations and the dispersive busyness of things.

We are not so certain. For us, the Self as the Greeks conceived it does not quite fit the story as we now tell it of how we are related to the world of phenomena, how we see ourselves, and how we present what we see to others. DNA, genetics, the brain as neuroscientists now describe it, have changed all that. And as our consciousness of things is extended further and further beyond the body's physical grasp, we become more and more conscious of the body itself, more attached and attentive to it; give more and more care to its preservation, its shape and look; keep closer track of what science, especially medical science, has to tell us of its mysterious workings. In an age when technological changes and discoveries that might once have taken centuries now happen in mere months, most of us have seen in a lifetime what might previously have taken several lifetimes to appear.

I am astonished when I look back to my own childhood by how little the body as it existed in the 1930s and 1940s resembles the body as it is today. Those were the years before antibiotics (penicillin), when people could still die by pricking their finger on a thorn and women in large numbers lost their lives in childbirth. When an epidemic like the Spanish flu could kill millions all around the globe in just months, and a single polio summer, such as 1947, could leave thousands of children and young adults, if they did not immediately succumb, crippled for life. A time before organ transplants, dialysis machines, heart by-passes, chemo; before the Pill. Before MRIs, pap smears, ultrasounds, angiograms. Before liposuction, breast implants, Botox, bionic ears and the spread throughout the community of a rigorous devotion to all the varieties of self-care, as the body became a blank sheet to be worked on and improved and decorated: diets, weights and aerobics, tattooing, waxing, piercing, the widespread phenomenon among teenagers of dental braces, and the cramming of pharmacy shelves with vitamin supplements, protein powders and pills for maintaining "friendly flora" in the gut.

The ideal image of the contemporary body, product of an obsession with "physique" and "tone" as well as vitality and good health, is flashed to us from the pages of glossy magazines and TV ads, through supermodels, sporting heroes, movie stars, soap stars, porn stars.

Freed at last of the identification of sensual pleasure with shame or sin, the body sees itself as being made for enjoyment but also for display. It is an advertisement, both to others and to ourselves, of an otherwise vague and unimaginable self, a product of make-up and make-over, of disciplined care, that is to be seen now as a moral as well as a physical achievement. At once carnal and innocent, it validates itself by being "attractive," and reaffirms its vigour and presence in full and healthy orgasm,[1] a phenomenon that in the half-century and more since Kinsey and Wilhelm Reich has become a matter for open discussion, and, since not all of us are equal to the ideal, for physical and psychological therapy. Failure now, either of image or performance, is the new shame; a source for some of new forms of humiliation and misery, and at the extreme, in anorexia and bulimia, of new forms of illness.

This preoccupation with body, though more widespread perhaps as a cultural phenomenon than ever before, is not quite new. What may be new is the way we have reconfigured our attitude to its end. To mortality. To death.

In the classical world, the death of the body meant the extinction of mind and body both, their dissolution into total nothingness. It was the fear of this nothingness that the schools had in mind, and hoped to cure, when they spoke of death. The arrival of Christianity brought a new solution, the survival of the soul in an afterlife; but this carried with it a new and more insidious fear, the fear of Judgment. With the promise of an afterlife of eternal bliss came the threat of eternal punishment.

And now?

For most of us the possibility of death or dying is no longer of immediate daily concern. The way we live now has seen to it that all this side of life and living is kept tidily out of sight. Dying is no longer a household occurrence. The old and the newborn no longer die at home. Except for the occasional horror of a road accident, dying is a managed affair of intensive-care units, clean, quiet, discretely isolated, where life-support systems glow and hum till they flatline and are turned off, then the piped music and tippy-toed formalities of the crematorium.

Our worst fear these days is not the finality and nothingness of death, or even the agony of dying— there are drugs to take care of that. It is that life may go on too long: to the point where we no longer have control of either our bodily or mental faculties and have slipped into the half-life, the virtual death-in-life, of that "second childhood and mere oblivion / Sans teeth, sans eyes, sans taste, sans everything" with which Jacques in *As You Like It* ends his account of our "strange eventful history."

Such a state would have been a rare one in Shakespeare's day, when the average life expectancy was less than forty; but he imagined or observed and was struck by it, and has left us this definitive description of what is now, for so many, a terrifying fact, and for the rest of us an equally terrifying possibility.

Yes, it is true we have little to complain of. Most of the conditions that might have made us "miserable" have been legislated for and ameliorated. But the externals that govern our lives seem more alien and impersonal in their new form than in the old.

One consequence of the Epimetheus version of our condition is that history is forever unfinished, forever in process; endless because our needs are endless. Technology until now has always met those needs and solved whatever problems it may have created along the way; that is what technology is for. But will it always do so?

Technology now has its own momentum and its own ends; the brain too is evolving, but not fast enough to keep up with what technology, each year, keeps pressing into our hands. Faced with the Planet (the Environment) on one side, with its various forms of globalisation, and on the other a room, as Pascal discovered, where we cannot be at peace, all we feel is a deeper sense of isolation and unease.

The Planet is a thing more remote and less manageable than the Earth.

The Earth was local crops and seasons, a kitchen garden that each day produced bread for the table, and olives and greens; it was dawn and sunset and age-old weather-rhymes: red sky at night, shepherd's delight, red sky at morning, shepherd's warning.

The Planet is a system that sustains us but is

dying, and whose slow death we worry over and feel responsible for—although it may only, in fact, be preparing another of its major disasters, one that might be fatal to us, and to many other forms of life, but would to the planet be no more than another phase in its accidental existence. We watch helplessly as the ice cap and the great glaciers melt. We fret over the possibility that the polar bear will disappear, or that the Gulf Stream may fail to do its work of warming Newfoundland and the British Isles. We watch the Amazon forests shrinking and the world's deserts rapidly expanding. We worry about food production and water as the population of the planet doubles in a century and is on its way to increasing by half again in even less.

Then, equally familiar, but also new in the role it is now seen to play in human behaviour, is that inner and increasingly mysterious agency the Brain, which has largely supplanted what Aristotle or Montaigne would have called the Mind.

No longer a jellylike mass of "grey matter," it has become a living thing, animal-like in its complex other life and workings. Its "areas," once as closed to view as "darkest Africa" in the nineteenth century, have now been fully mapped and can be viewed on a monitor. They light up in vivid colours to the stimulus of emotions—aggression or anger—or in response to such psychological states as depression and euphoria.

Mind was biddable. The Brain, it seems, is not. It goes its own way, determining our moods, preoccupied with its electrical pathways, with blood flow and the fluctuations of chemical or hormonal balance or imbalance, while we blunder about at its mercy and try to remain responsible for behaviours we may not entirely control.

As for the Economy, this new embodiment as I called it of Fate or the Gods, this global power that governs the lives of Chinese workers in village factories, Brazilian miners, children working cocoa plantations in West Africa, sex workers in Mumbai, real estate salesmen in Connecticut, sheep-farmers in Scotland or on the Darling Downs, disembodied voices in call centres in Bangalore, workers in the hospitality industry in Cancún or Venice or Fiji, keeping them fatefully interconnected, in its mysterious way, by laws that *do* exist, the experts assure us, though they cannot agree on what they are— it is too impersonal, too implacable for us to live comfortably with, or even to catch hold of and defy.

When we were in the hands of the Gods, we had

stories that made these distant beings human and brought them close. They got angry, they took our part or turned violently against us. They fell in love with us and behaved badly. They had their own problems and fought with one another, and like us were sometimes foolish. But their interest in us was personal. They watched over us and were concerned, though in moments of wilfulness or boredom they might also torment us as "wanton boys" do flies. We had our ways of obtaining their help as intermediaries. We could deal with them.

The Economy is impersonal. It lacks manageable dimensions. We have discovered no mythology to account for its moods. Our only source of information about it, the Media and their swarm of commentators, bring us "reports," but these do not help: a possible breakdown in the system, a new crisis, the descent on Greece, or Ireland or Portugal, like Jove's eagle, of the IMF. We are kept in a state of permanent low-level anxiety broken only by outbreaks of alarm.

Yes, we have little to complain of. But we are more stressed than ever, and safety seems even further out of reach.

The advanced and highly managed societies we live in today tend to assume that the good life, which can to a large extent be provided for, is at least a step on the way to the happy life, in that it removes so many of the conditions that might work against it. But the good life and the happy life, as I suggested earlier, belong to separate and in some ways unconnected meanings of happy; one refers to material fortune, which can be objectively measured, and the other to an interior state that cannot.

We are by nature measurers. We like to know how far we are from where we began, how far we have still to go.

When statisticians attempt to measure the "happiness coefficient" of a society—how much for how many—it is really the good life they are measuring, in such indicators as equality of opportunity, justice before the law, civil liberty, civil safety, economic stability, employment, food and housing, and of course all these are contributors to individual happiness. (Whether or not they are essential to it is another matter.) The trouble is that the statisticians can deal only with what can be generalised and yields itself to number.

But happiness is singular; each case speaks only for itself. It is also subjective. It belongs to the world of what is felt, what cannot be presented or numbered on a scale because it cannot be seen. It belongs to life as it is perceived from within by a single and singu-

lar woman or man, and we have only to consider for
a moment how inconsistent, how contradictory and
perverse any one of us can be, to see how difficult it is
to enter another man's feelings, especially about himself, and how impossible it might be, in the confusion
and mess in there, for even the man himself to say,
"I am happy."

All the conditions might be right, or seem so to
an outsider. But what if, like Sonya in *Uncle Vanya*,
you feel yourself to be "plain," essentially unlovely,
and for that reason or others unloveable? What if you
are in love and that love is not returned? What if you
lack, and are bitterly aware of it, the one talent that
might provide you with the best use of your energies
and the satisfaction of a life fulfilled? All of these are
personal feelings on which a man or woman's happiness might depend, and of which others could see
nothing.

When Protagoras, the Sophist of Plato's dialogue,
came up with what is perhaps the best known proposition in classical Greek thought, "Man is the measure
of all things," what he was declaring was that humanity is at the centre of the system we call Creation, and
that Man, with his particular qualities of reason, the

power of speech, the capacity to name and make and remake, is the point from which we must start in any enquiry we might undertake into the laws of the system, any exploration we might set out upon into the nature of knowing and being. But he was also pointing out the importance to our investigations of how one thing is related to another, of measure, or, as we are more likely to call it, proportion.

We start always from the body, and relate all things back to it. In a way that goes back to our most primitive beginnings, we use it to establish direction— where we are facing, where we might move to; to gauge distance—how far off an object is and how far we have got along the way towards it; to determine how each thing we are observing stands in relation to our own being—its size in relation to ours, how light or heavy it is when we try to lift it or weigh it on our palm; how much it occupies of the space we share; how it smells and tastes, how it feels to the touch or when we roll it between finger and thumb. We refer all this experience back to the body so that we can test against our senses the conclusions that observation and reasoning have led us to, and to see to what extent, in our understanding of these things, our sense of ourselves may have been changed and expanded.

This is how things must have been in our earliest

and most preliminary excursions into the world, for which we had in our calculations only the body as a source of measurement, and some shadow of all that is with us still.

These days we can travel around the globe at hundreds of kilometres an hour and project ourselves into space at several times that speed; but in some part of ourselves we are still bone-heavy creatures tied to the gravitational pull of the Earth, lumbering along as our great-grandfathers did, and the hundreds of generations before them, at four hundred paces an hour, and tiring.

(I happen to have set that sentence down in the old, slow way by hand. If I had used a computer, I might have got it down in a third, a quarter of the time. But like a good many writers, even this far into the twenty-first century, I find that the pace at which I work in longhand—at which my arm, my hand moves in the act of writing—has what is for me a "natural" relationship to the speed at which my mind works and I do not want to let go of a relationship that seems to be peculiarly mine. Writing by hand slows the thought process, allowing thinking to think again, mid-thought, and leaving open the possibility of second thoughts. It has an effect too on syntax, on the way a sentence gets shaped.)

It isn't a question of whether our mind can accommodate itself to new ways of seeing, to new technologies and realities that are abstract or virtual—clearly it can—but whether emotionally, psychologically, we can feel at home in a world whose dimensions so largely exceed, both in terms of the infinitely great and the infinitely small, what our bodies can keep in view; what we can imagine pacing out in a day's walk or reaching out to weigh in the palm of our hand, when with a radio telescope we can peer into the furthest reaches of the universe and a super-resolution microscope will allow us to watch a malaria parasite invading a human body cell.

One of the things the Greeks discovered, as early as the fifth century BC, is that the human body possesses perfect symmetry; all its parts reveal the same mathematical relationship of the smaller parts to the greater and of the greater to the whole; and what is true of the body is true of every part of creation, of plants and animals, and of Creation as a whole. All this, in the case of the body, is laid out clearly for us in Leonardo's image of Vitruvian Man.

Created in the late fifteenth century but deriving from the best known writer on classical architecture, the Roman Vitruvius,[2] it shows a naked man simultaneously inscribed, once standing and once with his

arms outflung and his legs parted to form an equi-
lateral triangle, in both a circle and a square. It is
a study in measure, in proportion; in which all the
smaller parts of the body, fingers, palms, feet etc., are
mathematically related to the larger, and the larger,
breadth of shoulder for example, which is a fourth of
body-height, to the whole. So the palm is the width
of four fingers, the length of the foot is four palms,
the space between the outstretched arms is equal to
the figure's height, which is twenty-four palms.

This symmetry within the body was to the Greeks
important in itself, but more important still was the
relationship of this part also to the whole; of the
body—our bodies—to the whole of creation, whose
symmetry we reproduce and share. For the Greeks,
this perfect harmony they had discovered, between
Man and the world he was in, was mystical, but was
grounded in the verifiable facts of mathematics.

The Golden Section, as it is now called, became
the basis of the classical orders of architecture, later
of medieval cathedrals, and has been made use of by
painters, sculptors, architects and technical designers
of every sort right down to the present. The body is
still our measure. Somehow what exceeds its grasp,
even if our mind and imagination can go there, makes
us uneasy, sets us anxiously adrift in a dimensionless

faces he needs to read, individual quirks he must take note of and learn to negotiate. But within the *limits*—though he has not chosen them—he can, moment by moment, one day at a time, make this life work for him, and find not settled contentment and rest—how can any of us find that?—but a kind of happiness he can make do with from one day to the next.

world where we lose all sense of where body—the *sensory* body we are contained in—either begins or ends.

The fact is, a man can be happy in even the most miserable conditions if the world he is in, and has to deal with, still has what he feels to be "human" dimensions; is still proportionate to what his body can recognise and encompass.

I go back, in this set of shifting perspectives, to the extreme case of Shukhov, at the end of the one day in his life that Solzhenitsyn has so immediately, and densely and intimately, created for us.

Shukhov has no reason in the world to be happy. The conditions of his life constitute the most terrible form we can imagine of modern misery: a prisoner of the state in the wastes of Siberia with no rights of any kind; reduced to a number in a camp; freezing, half-starved and with little hope of seeing out his sentence. But as we see him at the end of his day, settling down to sleep and preparing for the next of his three thousand, six hundred and fifty-three days of forced labour, he *is* happy, and he tells us so. For all the conditions that have been created—deliberately, officially—to break his spirit and keep him miserable, he is "content," as so many of us who enjoy the good life and ought to be are not.

Unlikely as it may seem, Shukhov is our perfect

example of the happy man. And we understand his state, and believe him when he tells us he is happy, because we have lived through this day with him.

Fiction, with its preference for what is small and might elsewhere seem irrelevant; its facility for smuggling us into another skin and allowing us to live a new life there; its painstaking devotion to what without it might go unnoticed and unseen; its respect for contingency, and the unlikely and odd; its willingness to expose itself to moments of low, almost animal being and make them nobly illuminating, can deliver truths we might not otherwise stumble on.

Shukhov is not happy because he has solved the problem of "how to live"—the life he lives is too provisional, too makeshift for that. Or because, as the classical schools would have put it, he has achieved self-containment, self-sufficiency. Quite the opposite.

What he achieves, briefly, intermittently, is moments of self-fulfilment, something different and more accessible, more democratic we might call it, than self-containment. But he achieves it only at moments.

He is happy *now*—who can know what tomorrow or the day after will do to him? He is happy *within limits*—and this may be a clue to what makes happiness possible for him, or for any of us.

For all the scope, both of time and space, that con-

temporary forms of knowledge have made available to us, what we can fully comprehend—that is, have direct sensory experience of—remains small; and only with what we have fully comprehended and feel at home in do we feel safe.

What is human is what we can keep track of. In terms of space this means what is within sight, what is local and close; within reach, within touch.

What most alarms us in our contemporary world, what unsettles and scares us, is the extent to which the forces that shape our lives are no longer personal—they know nothing of us; and to the e that we know nothing of them—cannot put to them, cannot find in them anything we as human—we cannot deal with them. small, powerless creatures in the coil ible monster, vast but insubstantial, grasped or wrestled with.

Compared with this, Shukho its harshness, is entirely huma the limits of his grasp if no *can* deal with it.

He takes short views ? est units of time—a fe a stretch of space paces, a thousand

Notes

The Character of a Happy Life

1. Alexander Solzhenitsyn, *One Day in the Life of Ivan Denisovich*, trans. Gillon Aitken, 1971.
2. Montaigne, *Essais,* "Of Solitude," trans. E. J. Trenchmann, 1929.
3. Horace's *Second Epode*, "Beatus ille qui" has been a favourite text for translators and imitators in English, providing as it does a rich account of the joys of country living and of retirement from the world of affairs. Ben Johnson's version, "The Praises of Country Life" from *Under-wood* (completed 1616) stays close to the original and preserves Horace's final stroke of irony: that these are the words of the usurer, Alphius, who has now got his money in on the Ides and can pursue the pleasant fantasy of retirement and the life of a gentleman farmer till he is ready to put his money to use again on the Kalens. Wotton, writing sometime in the 1620s, takes the poem out of the mouth of Alphius and plays it straight. The version of the poem that comes seventy years later, from the hand of the twelve-year-old Alexander Pope:

> Happy the man whose wish and care
> A few paternal acres bound,
> Content to breathe his native air
> In his own ground, etc.

has become the classic statement in English of an ideal country existence and a life that has fulfilled its round in perfect simplicity and goodness.
4. Wotton's poems, with a Life by Izaak Walton, were published as *Reliquae Wottonianae* in 1651, twelve years after his death.
5. Montaigne, *Essais*, ibid.

"The Pursuit of Happiness"

1. This was Jefferson's original formulation. He showed the draft to John Adams and Benjamin Franklin, who suggested that "sacred and undeniable" should become "self-evident." The draft was then submitted to the Continental Congress, where to Jefferson's chagrin the latter part, the indictment of the King, was considerably amended. In the earlier part the only change was the deletion of "inherent and" in the phrase "inherent and undeniable right."
2. Jefferson, in a letter to Richard Henry Lee, 8 May 1825.
3. Mason's preamble was adopted by the Virginia Convention in Williamsburg on 12 June and published in the *Pennsylvania Gazette* on the same day. If Jefferson had not already seen it in draft he would certainly have read it there. The committee meeting of Congress (John Adams, Jefferson, Franklin, Robert Livingstone, Roger Sherman) at which Jefferson and Adams were delegated to draft the Declaration, had taken place the day before. Jefferson wrote the Declaration (in just "a day or two" according to Adams) during the following week, and with Adams's and Franklin's amendments it went to the Continental Congress on 28 June; the Congress debated it on 2 July. On 4 July the Congress approved its revisions and the Declaration went to the printer.

Unrest

1. Heidegger's use of the *Protagoras*, and his thoughts on technology, are the subject of a documentary film on the Danube, *The Ister* (Black Box Sound and Image, 2004, 2005, 187 min.), by David Barison and Daniel Ross. It takes its title from Heidegger's 1942 lectures on a poem, "Der Ister," by the German Romantic poet Heinrich Hölderlin; Ister being the name by which the Danube was known to the Greeks and Romans.
2. George Herbert (1593–1633) was the parish priest of the village of Bremerton in Wiltshire. His poems, which he describes as "a picture of the many spiritual conflicts that have passed between God and my soul, before I could subject mine to the will of Jesus

my Master, in whose service I have now found perfect freedom," were circulated in manuscript among his friends but not published during his lifetime. He left them in the hands of his friend and fellow-cleric, Nicholas Ferrar, founder of the religious community at Little Gidding, who published them under the title *The Temple* in 1633, just months after Herbert's death.

3. Pascal, *Pensées*, no 139, *Divertissement*: "J'ai découvert que tout le malheur des hommes vient d'une seule chose, qui est de ne savoir demeurer en répos, dans une chambre."

4. Condorcet, Marie Jean Antoine Nicolas de Caritat (1743–94), *Esquisse d'un tableau historique des progrès de l'esprit humain*, published 1795, trans. June Barraclough, 1955.

Happiness in the Flesh

1. Ovid's *Ars Amatoria* was published in 1 AD and its notoriety and wide success was no doubt one factor in the decision of the Emperor Augustus, in 8 AD, to banish him to the furthest limits of the empire at Tomis on the Black Sea coast, near what is now Constanza. Ovid was never pardoned, and the nature of his death, and the site of his grave, somewhere in Scythia, became one of the haunting mysteries of the next fifteen or more centuries. His poems, the *Metamorphoses*, but even more his erotic poems, *Amores* and *Ars Amatoria*, became models, both in the Mediaeval period and the Renaissance, for "imitation" and the discovery of new ways of writing and living. The *Ars Amatoria*, with its vividly pictorial presentation of the ancient myths, became the source of innumerable paintings by Titian, Rubens, Poussin, Breugel ("The Fall of Icarus") and others. The persona and voice Ovid created in his poem, that of the professional lover, the metropolitan rake and devil-may-care, frequenter of street-stalls, alleyways, theatres, always on the make and speaking, even in his love-talk, the language of the streets, is taken up by poets in half a dozen European languages, and in English by all the writers of love poems from Donne to Lovelace, Suckling and Waller.

2. The sixteen sonnets that make up Aretino's *Sonetti Lussuriosi* were written between 1525 and 1527 as a pendant to a scandal of the

year before, when Marco Antonio Raimondo engraved and published a set of erotic drawings by Giulio Romano. Raimondo was
arrested by the Roman authorities and when Aretino protested on
his behalf, the poet was forced to flee. The engravings, and the
drawings on which they were based, have disappeared.

3. Donne, "The Sunne Rising": "call countrey ants to harvest offices."
   The reference is to the fable of the Ant and the Grasshopper.

4. Donne, "Elegie: To his Mistriss Going to Bed." This is one of five
   elegies entered among Donne's *Poems* in the Stationer's Register
   in 1632 but withheld from publication in the first edition of 1633,
   presumably on the grounds of their indecency. The John Donne
   who wrote them, recently deceased, was the pious and highly-
   respected Dr. Donne, Dean of St. Paul's, author of the "Holy Sonnets" and some hundred sermons, favourite preacher at the Court
   of James I, and the divine chosen by his successor, Charles I,
   to preach the first sermon of his reign. Eighty of Donne's sermons,
   which he had left as a legacy to his son, were printed in 1640,
   together with the first version of the poet's *Life* (there were to be
   three others) by his friend Izaak Walton.

5. Rubens' first wife, Isabella Brant, had died at the age of thirty-five
   in 1629, after seventeen years of marriage. In the early days of
   their marriage, in 1610, he had painted a portrait of them seated
   side by side in their garden in Antwerp; very formally dressed—
   both hatted and he sporting a magnificent lace collar, she an
   equally elegant ruff, her right hand resting on his left, his right
   hand curled loosely on the hilt of his sword. Two young people—
   he was twenty-nine, she just eighteen—looking out, wonderfully
   at home with one another, from their calm and richly-appointed
   world. Rubens was devastated by his loss, but recovered in his
   stoical way. Four years later he married Helena Fourment, the
   daughter of an Antwerp silk-merchant.

6. Born just thirteen years after Shakespeare, about whom we know
   almost nothing, Rubens is more visible, and his life more fully
   documented, than all but a few princes of his time. In an age
   when religion was a matter of life and death—his father was a
   Calvinist, Rubens himself an exemplary Counter-Reformation
   Catholic—he seems to have been naturally pious but in every way
   open-minded. Like his brother Philip he was a latter-day Stoic of

the school of Seneca. For the last two decades of his life Europe was ravaged by the most violent conflict the continent would know till the wars of the twentieth century, the Thirty Years War of 1618 to 1648. Rubens was personally acquainted with most of the participants, princes, kings, emperors, and was a trusted diplomat, travelling constantly between Antwerp, London, Paris and Madrid as a bearer of conditions for treaties and proposals of one kind or another for peace. Two of his greatest allegorical paintings depict the horrors of War and the promise of Peace. Within all this public activity—in his grand house in Antwerp and later on his country estate, the Chateau of Steen, where in retirement at last from his public duties, and in the happiness of his second marriage, he devoted himself to painting a hundred and twenty scenes from Ovid for the Torre de Parada in Spain and half a dozen visions of the earthly paradise based on the local countryside—his personal and domestic life appears to have been extraordinarily serene.

7. William Wordsworth, *Preface to Lyrical Ballads*, 1798: "Poetry is the spontaneous overflow of powerful feelings; it takes its origin from emotion recollected in tranquility; the emotion is contemplated till, by a species of reaction, the tranquility gradually disappears, and an emotion kindred to that which was before the subject of contemplation, is gradually produced, and does actually exist in the mind. In this mood successful production generally begins . . ."

The Way We Live Now

1. "Orgasm" entered the language as a physiological term in the late seventeenth century but became socially acceptable, and widely used, only in the early 1950s, after the publication of Alfred C. Kinsey's *Sexual Behavior in the Human Male* (1948) and *Sexual Behavior in the Human Female* (1953). Wilhelm Reich's *The Function of the Orgasm*, first published in German in 1927, translated and published in the United States in 1942, became one of the most fashionable reference books of the sexual revolution of the 1960s.

2. *De architectura,* a treatise in ten volumes on architecture, hydrau-

lics, mathematics, building techniques, decoration and town planning, by the Roman architect and engineer Marcus Vitruvius Pollio was the classical text to which all the major architects of the Renaissance turned for what Nicholas Pevsner calls "the divine order and perspective" of the classical world, but also for the lost secrets of its technology.

David Malouf is the author of eleven novels, a collection of stories, a memoir, three opera libretti, and many collections of poetry. Awards he has received include the inaugural Australia-Asia Literary Award, the International IMPAC Dublin Literary Award, the Prix Femina Étranger, and the Los Angeles Times Book Award. He lives in Australia.

A NOTE ON THE TYPE

This book was set in Adobe Garamond. Designed for the
Adobe Corporation by Robert Slimbach, the fonts are based
on types first cut by Claude Garamond (c. 1480–1561).
Garamond was a pupil of Geoffroy Tory and is believed to
have followed the Venetian models, although he introduced
a number of important differences, and it is to him that we
owe the letter we now know as "old style."

Composed by North Market Street Graphics,
Lancaster, Pennsylvania

Printed and bound by Berryville Graphics,
Berryville, Virginia

Designed by M. Kristen Bearse